Encounter:

ADVENT REFLECTIONS
FOR CATHOLICS IN TRANSITION

ANNA SCHULTEN

Scripture texts in this work are taken from the *New American Bible, revised edition* © 2010, 1991, 1986, 1970 Confraternity of Christian Doctrine, Washington, D.C.

ISBN: 1978150490
ISBN-13: 978-1978150492

To my Love and all military personnel who spend the season apart from their loved ones.

May this time of reflection help us grow in faith and love despite the distance.

I love you, my beautiful one.

Contents

Quick Start

If it's not yet Advent or if you'd like to learn a little more, check out the introduction section on the following pages.

If you're getting started a bit late and you want to jump right in, here are the basics you need to know:

- **Read at your own pace.** There are four reflections per week. Read them on the days that work best for you.

- **Guided scripture meditations.** Each week includes the past Sunday's readings so you can continue living the Word during the week. You can also read the readings in advance, if you find that more helpful.

- **Before Mass.** Each week includes a few reflections to sum up the week before you head to Mass for the weekend.
- **Bonus material.** Service, Advent traditions, and other tidbits to enrich your season are explained in the introduction.

That's it! Head over to page 32.

Introduction

Indiana, Alaska, Ministry, Military. What do all these things have in common?

They all mark points of great transition in my life. They're all places God spoke to me through everyday challenges.

I don't claim to know what kinds of transitions you're going through. I don't know what changes and challenges you're experiencing, and I will never know the kind of stress you're under.

This book isn't a magic bullet, and it doesn't pretend to be.

This book is an opportunity for grounding, even when our lives are sideways or upside down. They're the stories of real life, real experiences, and God's presence in the everyday reality of our lives. These readings and reflections will be here whenever you need them. Use them as much or as little as you need; the important thing is that we're continuing the journey.

I'm also praying for you, and for anyone who may read this book down the road. Whether you know me or not, know that you're on my mind, and that I've been praying for you. God is cool like that.

Think about the transitions you're going through in your life. The important thing to note is that God is present in your transitions. He's here with you, always present-closer than the air you breathe.

He knows what you're going through.

Even more, he's been through it. Our God is fully human, and fully divine. He has walked our world. He knows heartbreak, and change, and loss, and betrayal. He does not leave us alone in these times. He is always present, even when we can't feel him.

This Advent, as you encounter changes and transitions in your life, encounter Christ. He is with you, today and always.

We Wait in Joyful Hope

I'm one of those dedicated "no-Christmas-before-Thanksgiving" people.

Every year, it's always the same. Decorations arrive a bit earlier, trees are up a bit sooner, and before you know it, Christmas products are on the shelves in early October. Commercialism has trampled Halloween's toes in its rush to "winter holiday cheer." I have a friend who's ready to deck the halls come September, but I just... I can't. It's too soon. It doesn't sit right with me.

While my neighbors are hanging lights and anchoring plastic nativity scenes in the front yard, I'm mourning the loss of a shortened autumn. Hot chocolate with peppermint is about as festive as I get until December 20th or so.

I suppose that means my "no-Christmas-before-Thanksgiving" stance is more extreme than I thought. I'm one of those "no-Christmas-before-Christmas" people, if we're being honest. I change the radio station mid-December when holly jolly Christmas songs come on before their time.

Am I a Scrooge? I suppose some people would call me that, and with plenty of evidence to back it up. But there's something greater coming than clearance sales. I hate to miss Advent due to the hustle-and-bustle of commercialized Christmas. There is enough busy in the world. For once in a season, we have the chance to take a break, spend some time in the quiet, and prepare our hearts for an encounter with Jesus.

When I reflect on Advent, two phrases come to mind. "Prepare the way of the Lord" is the first, reminiscent of John the Baptist's call for our conversion. "Waiting in joyful hope" is the second: words taken from the liturgy. This booklet aims to do both of these things: prepare, and wait.

This book veers from the traditional daily Advent reflection guide in a few ways. While each week includes reflection readings, it recognizes we may not have the time to read a reflection every single day. Rather than despairing because of a busy lifestyle, I encourage you to make this book your own, and work through it at your own pace.

Finally, this book includes white space and lined paper for your own reflections. I encourage you to use it and actually write in this book. Don't worry about preserving its mint condition (because that's what I would do; I'm writing to myself here). If you intend to read it again in three years, you can buy another copy for less than a fast-food meal with a cup of fancy coffee. If nothing else, at the very least, pick up a blank companion journal to keep with this book.

Make this Advent personal. Take notes. Underline. Write. Doodle in the margins. But as the author, I don't expect you to leave this book in pristine condition for the next reader. Use it as a tool to explore your faith and to encounter Christ this season. He is here and he is reaching out to each one of us.

This Advent, prepare your heart for our Lord. When he knocks at the door, let him in.

Advent Traditions

One of my favorite Advent traditions is definitely the Advent wreath. Call me a pyromaniac, but I love candles and their symbolism.

My in-laws light Advent candles during mealtimes throughout the season, until the purple ones burn down to little nubs and the pink one has no way to catch up. What if the pink candle was already smaller than the rest? Wouldn't that work out a little better?

Advent, like most of the other major holidays, reminds me of church decorating. Advent was second only to Lent in its simplicity: the church is empty except for the Advent wreath. Granted, our wreath is gigantic, or at least it always seemed to be so when I was a little child. Three feet is a large enough diameter for the whole church. Different families took turns lighting the proper candles during the weekend Masses. It was a nice touch to the season: family, within community, sharing the light of Christ.

Growing in faith requires more than simple knowledge. We know facts and context about our faith, sure, but we also experience Church through the five senses. We speak, and sing, we listen, we smell, we touch, we taste.

And not just on Sundays.

As you prepare for Advent, whether you're preparing with a family or on your own, here are a few ways to make the season tangible.

Mass.

If you're not going to Mass every week, now is the prime time to encounter Christ in the Liturgy. The Mass is the Source and Summit of our faith: everything comes from it, and everything points back to it.

If you already go to Mass every weekend, try to go to Mass during one of the weekday services. My life has taken on a whole new meaning since a priest challenged me to begin attending daily Mass. When I worked my day around that time with God, I began to put other parts of my life in order as well.

Reconciliation

Many parishes offer a Reconciliation Service beyond their usual confession times during Advent. Take time to go to the Sacrament of Reconciliation and encounter Christ's healing, mercy, and peace.

Open the Word

God speaks to us through the scripture along with the sacraments. I've never been good at reading the Bible on a daily or weekly basis, but I find it easier to read scripture when I use the Sunday readings as a guide.

I've provided the Sunday readings for Cycle B (2017, 2020, etc.) in this book, alternating with the weekly reflections. It may be even better to open up a hard copy Bible, leaf through it, and read the readings there. You'll have a better context for the readings, and you'll get the added benefit of footnotes and cross-references.

The Advent Wreath

Every Catholic church has an Advent wreath during Advent: three purple candles and a pink one. At Christmas, we also add a white "Light of Christ" candle in the center. Each candle represents one of the weeks of Advent, along with its theme:

- Week One: Purple: Hope
- Week Two: Purple: Faith
- Week Three: Pink: Joy
- Week Four: Purple: Peace

Buy or make an Advent wreath for your own home, and light its candles during meal times or special times of prayer. Seasonal prayers and small prayer services are available online to go along with your Advent wreath. To bring things full circle, you can read these reflections by the light of an Advent wreath.

A Manger for Baby Jesus.

One of the simplest Advent traditions is to prepare a manger for Jesus. Every time you do a good deed or make a small sacrifice, place a piece of straw or strip of paper in his manger. It's a simple, tangible way to recognize the way our actions connect to preparing for Christ's coming.

Jesse Tree

This one has its roots in the stories of the Old Testament. You can buy a set of Jesse Tree ornaments, or you can make your own. Find a set you like and spend time each day reflecting on the characters that make up salvation history.

Advent Calendar

Calendars are as varied as Jesse Trees: you can find themes of everything from chocolate, to storybooks, to service projects, to wine. Some calendars are more spiritual than others, there's no doubt about that. Nonetheless, an Advent calendar acts as a tangible countdown for the season.

Each of these traditions invites you to walk with the whole church as we prepare our hearts for Christ.

How is God calling you to pray with us this season? Take a minute to review this chapter and pick a tradition or two you'd like to try this Advent.

Service

I have a love/hate/love relationship with service projects, especially ones that involve one-on-one outreach.

I planned a mission trip to Jamaica with some high school students from my church. We were going to work with children and young adults with disabilities. I have family and friends with a range of mental disabilities, and though I was a little nervous, I knew it would all work out. Probably.

It was my first time traveling out of country, so that was exciting enough. But when we arrived and met the children, I had an instant paralysis of fear. Who was I, to think I could volunteer here? What in the world did I have to offer? I'm an introvert. This is crazy!

But I put on a brave face and jumped in with both feet. We started work with the children and everything changed. I fell in love with them, their joy, their kindness. They loved us, even when we were uncomfortable and not sure what to do.

My preferred method of service has always been creative and behind-the-scenes. I like to make things. I like to craft, and labor, and design, and share. But I know God is calling me to push beyond my comfort zone.

Every time I take part in outreach service, it goes something like this. I get excited, and I invite my friends. I am thrilled by the prospect of the difference I'll make in someone's life.

And then I arrive at the destination, and fall into some weird form of stage fright. No, I'm not performing. I'm not even on stage, or in the public eye. But I have a paralyzing moment of fear: why did I ever decide to do this? Whose idea was this, anyway? Oh, that's right. Mine.

Once I get over the initial interaction and begin volunteering, everything is easy. I have a great time, and I have no idea why I was so nervous. And I make plans to come back again.

Jesus continues to call us to make our faith real through service. We must serve the poor, the vulnerable, the marginalized. It's our job to give back to the community and support one another. It's a key part to our salvation (check out Matthew chapter 25, or the book of James on the importance of faith and works).

This section provides a few service project ideas that correspond to Advent themes. Try to think of some ways in your life you can share hope, faith, joy, and peace with others this Advent.

Fill a shoebox care package.

Provide gifts, supplies, and Christmas cheer to soldiers or children in need. It's a creative and quick way to give back. Even young children can help and learn the value of giving.

Donate gently-used winter gear to a local shelter.

This is especially helpful for people who live in a colder climate. You can also offer these items- hats, gloves, coats, socks- to people in need, if you encounter them on a one-on-one basis.

Call or meet with a friend who is having a hard time.

Check in with them, in person if possible, and give them the time and space to share what's on their mind. Listen to them. A listening heart is one of the greatest gifts of hope you can give.

Ask for prayer requests.

Before I go to Adoration each week, I ask my social media network if anyone has any prayer requests. It's a simple, non-intrusive way to share my faith, and to reach out to my friends and family.

Little acts go a long way.

Make it your mission to do little acts of kindness with great love, as St. Therese said. Hold open the door. Leave a quarter in a convenience store vending machine. Pay for the person behind you in a fast food drive-through line. The options are limitless.

Letters of Love.

When you're preparing a Christmas card for someone, add in a little note of why this person means so much to you. And tell them you love them. Words have power. We build each other up.

Connect with a friend or family member.

The next time you're out to eat with a friend or spending time with someone, make them the center of your time. Put your phone on vibrate or silent. Make eye contact. Listen. Ask lots of questions. Take a step out of the digital world we live in, and be a good friend in the here and now.

Your ideas here:

_____

_____

_____

_____

_____

_____

Scripture

Catholics get a bad rap when it comes to scripture. Most Catholics would agree to the stereotype: we don't know scripture very well. We're not well-versed in the Bible, pun intended.

Luckily, quoting chapter and verse is only a part of knowing scripture. Our problem is we can't see the forest for all the trees, per se.

We immerse ourselves in scripture every Sunday, even if we don't realize it. The vast majority of the Mass is scriptural, and what isn't scriptural is part of our tradition. Granted, most Catholics don't know where in the Bible they'd find such references to stories we know well. But at least it's a step in the right direction.

How should I pray with scripture?

The hardest part about praying with scripture is getting started. There are many books and resources available to help you along your way, but the easiest way I've found is through Lectio Divina.

Lectio Divina: What is it?

It's an ancient Christian tradition: holy readings, a way to encounter Christ in the word. Rather than reading the Bible straight through from beginning to end, Lectio Divina is a bit slower, and a bit more intentional. It takes scripture piece by piece, section by section, and gives us the space to get familiar with the stories. There are a few variations to the process, but here is the most basic structure:

- **Lectio.** First, invite the Holy Spirit to be present with you during your reading. Then read the passage, and listen for a word or phrase that stands out to you. It could be something that catches your attention, or a part that surprises or confuses you.
- **Meditatio.** Read the reading again, and ask God what he's trying to say to you through the reading. How is God speaking to you?
- **Oratio.** Read the passage a third time, and respond to God. What do you have to say to him? What will you change in your life in response to God's word?

· **Contemplatio**. Read the passage one final time. Take a moment of silence and thank God for the time you've spent with him.

Yep, you counted that right: altogether, you'll read the same passage four times. Yes, it takes time, and yes, getting to know the word of the Lord is worth the time it takes.

Each week of this book includes three separate readings from Sunday Mass. The first reading is from the Old Testament; it's followed by an Epistle (a letter) from the New Testament and completed by a Gospel reading. Each reading also includes a Lectio Divina guide and journaling or reflection prompts. I encourage you to take notes on your reflection time in this book, or in a separate journal, or even in your Bible.

Pre-Advent Meditation

The following Gospel reading is from the last Sunday of the liturgical year, the Sunday before Advent, the Solemnity of Our Lord Jesus Christ, King of the Universe.

MATTHEW 25: 31-46 – CYCLE A

Jesus said to his disciples: "When the Son of Man comes in his glory, and all the angels with him, he will sit upon his glorious throne, and all the nations will be assembled before him. And he will separate them one from another, as a shepherd separates the sheep from the goats. He will place the sheep on his right and the goats on his left. Then the king will say to those on his right, 'Come, you who are blessed by my Father. Inherit the kingdom prepared for you from the foundation of the world. For I was hungry and you gave me food, I was thirsty and you gave me drink, a stranger and you welcomed me, naked and you clothed me, ill and you cared for me, in prison and you visited me.' Then the righteous will answer him and say, 'Lord, when did we see you hungry and feed you, or thirsty and give you drink? When did we see you a stranger and welcome you, or naked and clothe you? When did we see you ill or in prison, and visit you?' And the king will say to them in reply, 'Amen, I say to you, whatever you did for one of the least brothers of mine, you did for me.' Then he will say to those on his left, 'Depart from me, you accursed, into the eternal fire prepared for the devil and his angels. For I was hungry and you gave me no food, I was thirsty and you gave me no drink, a stranger and you gave me no welcome, naked and you gave me no clothing, ill and in prison, and you did not care for me.' Then they will answer and say, 'Lord, when did we see you hungry or thirsty or a stranger or naked or ill or in prison, and not minister to your needs?' He will answer them, 'Amen, I say to you, what you did not do for one of these least ones, you did not do for me.' And these will go off to eternal punishment, but the righteous to eternal life."

Lectio Divina:

- Invite the Holy Spirit to be with you.
- **Lectio:** What word or phrase stands out?
- **Meditatio:** What is God saying to you today?
- **Oratio:** What do you have to say to God? How will your life change because of this passage?
- **Contemplatio:** thank God in silence.

Questions for Reflection:

- When is it hard to be a sheep? When is it easy to be a goat?

_____

_____

_____

_____

- Which corporal work of mercy is your favorite? Which one do you find most challenging?

_____

_____

_____

_____

- Have you ever experienced God's presence through service? How did it impact you? How were the people you were serving impacted?

_____

_____

_____

_____

Journaling space:

_____

_____

_____

_____

_____

_____

_____

_____

_____

_____

—

Pre-Advent Reflection

Jot down a few notes on the following questions below.

- Imagine that it's Christmas day. How do you want to be different? What parts of your life do you hope will have grown or changed?

        _____

        _____

        _____

        _____

- How will you give back to the community this week?

_____

_____

_____

_____

- What Advent traditions will you take part in?

_____

_____

_____

_____

Before you go to Mass on the First Sunday of Advent:
- Who/what will you pray for?

_____

_____

_____

_____

- Week 1 Homily Notes:

_____

_____

_____

_____

Weekly Reflections

Week 1: Hope

If ever there was a season when we need hope, it is today.

I asked my junior high students to list some "storms" in our world today, both literal and metaphorical. We jumped from wildfires and names of hurricanes, to nationwide shootings and local violent crimes, to large-scale symptoms of global ill: greed, poverty, and anger.

My junior high students aren't the only ones capable of naming the brokenness of our world. Everyone is bearing his or her own cross. Even if it's not something visible, everyone has that one "thing" in their lives. That one bit of suffering. For a lot of us, there are several "things" in our lives. They try our patience, break our hearts, and overwhelm us.

But there is hope. There is always hope.

I love being Catholic in part because of our understanding of redemptive suffering. We can unite our suffering with Jesus for the benefit of others. Maybe it's the special intention of a family member or a friend in need. Maybe it's something you're struggling with in your own life. Either way, big or small, God can use our suffering to benefit others.

Our brokenness is not for nothing: we can use it to build up each other. As Saint Paul says, my strength is made perfect in my weakness (2 Corinthians 12: 9). He also says in (Colossians 1: 24) that our sufferings make up for what is lacking in the suffering of Christ.

It's not a nice metaphor or nice words. This is a real deal. Our suffering can give strength to those in need. Of course, we don't go looking for suffering... but it always finds us. It's a part of the broken world we live in. As we encounter these sufferings, rather than fleeing from them, let's embrace our crosses and carry them: for Christ, and for those we love.

As we begin this journey of Advent, let's take a minute to gather some petitions weighing on our hearts. Write them down here so you don't forget them. Abbreviations and generalities are fine; you know in your heart who you're praying for.

Make a commitment to pray for these people throughout the weeks to come. Even better, make a commitment to offer your sufferings for them. As you encounter brokenness, offer it to God for these people.

Petitions:

Who will you offer your sufferings for? What are your personal, family, friend, or community needs? Who is in most need in our world today?

_____

_____

_____

_____

Sufferings to Offer:

To some degree, we can each anticipate some of our sufferings and struggles. List a few of them here. Which sufferings would you like to offer up for people in need?

_____

_____

_____

_____

Strength for the Journey:

Reflect on the challenges and transitions you're facing. Who are five people you can contact for support?

_____

_____

_____

_____

A Prayer for Transitions

Lord, you know my heart.
You know the challenges I face.
Walk with me today.
Help me to face each adversity with courage
and to embrace my cross with grace.
May I fight the good fight
for the glory of your kingdom.
Through Christ our Lord.
Amen.

Scripture: First Reading

ISAIAH 63: 16B-17, 19B; 64: 2-7 – CYCLE B

You, LORD, are our father, our redeemer, you are named from of old. Why do you make us wander, LORD, from your ways, and harden our hearts so that we do not fear you? Return for the sake of your servants, the tribes of your heritage. Oh, that you would rend the heavens and come down, with the mountains quaking before you, while you worked awesome deeds we could not hope for, such as had not been heard of from of old. No ear has ever heard, no eye ever seen, any God but you working such deeds for those who wait for him. Would that you might meet us doing right, that we might be mindful of you in our ways! Indeed, you are angry; we have sinned, we have acted wickedly. We have all become like something unclean, all our just deeds are like polluted rags; we have all withered like leaves, and our crimes carry us away like the wind. There are none who call upon your name, none who rouse themselves to take hold of you; for you have hidden your face from us and have delivered us up to our crimes. Yet, LORD, you are our father; we are the clay and you our potter: we are all the work of your hand.

Lectio Divina:

- Invite the Holy Spirit to be with you.
- **Lectio:** What word or phrase stands out?
- **Meditatio:** What is God saying to you today?
- **Oratio:** What do you have to say to God? How will your life change because of this passage?
- **Contemplatio:** thank God in silence.

Questions for Reflection:

- What's your favorite image of God from this passage? Why does it stand out to you?

_____

_____

_____

_____

- Despite our failures, God reaches out to us. Reflect on a time God gave you forgiveness. What happened? How did it change you?

  _____

  _____

  _____

  _____

-

- What does it mean to be the clay in God's hands? How does this idea affect your daily life?

  _____

  _____

  _____

  _____

Journaling space:

Journey

I never knew how much I loved to travel until I made my first trip out of state.

My boyfriend (who would become my husband) completed military training on two different bases, several hours from home. I traveled to both parts of the country for his graduation ceremonies, first with my in-laws, and second with my parents.

Each journey was a long drive, but a worthwhile adventure. I was able to see a new part of the country and spend time with my boyfriend; that alone was worth the long drives in fancy rental cars.

Still, I grew up a small-town country girl, and I liked it that way, thank you very much. I had intended to grow up in the same county, or at least the same region, and spend my whole life surrounded by cornfields, rolling hills, and patches of woods.

But God was calling me to something different.

When my boyfriend-turned-husband and I decided to get married, we knew that the military would be the key factor in determining where we would live. Uncle Sam would choose our destination, or the first in a series of several destinations. Besides the road trips and the odd conference or vacation, I knew nothing of the rest of the world.

I had lived in the same house my entire life. The first time I ever moved (besides in and out of college dorm rooms) was when my husband called and told me we would be moving to the Last Frontier. I still remember where I was when he told me: at a Barnes and Noble in my hometown. I wandered over to the travel books section to see if they had any books on Alaska. They didn't.

Given the longest road trip I'd ever done was 12 hours, I couldn't- and still can't really- fathom the distance that is 4,000 miles. I had never dreamed of traveling to Alaska, much less moving there for at least three years on the government's dime. I knew nothing about Alaska, and no one who lived there.

When we stepped onto that first plane, as much as my heart was breaking, leaving everything familiar, I knew that God had a plan for us. We were together, he was with us, and that's what mattered.

I imagine that's how Mary felt as she left her hometown to travel to Bethlehem. She didn't know what the journey held in store, but God was with her, as was her husband, and that was enough.

The journey can be overwhelming, even terrifying, but it's a step on the way to a new life, a new phase, a new mindset. A new relationship. This Advent, I hope we're able to enter into the journey to encountering Christ this season.

Questions for Reflection:

- What's the longest journey you've ever taken? What did you learn from it?

  _____

  _____

  _____

  _____

- Where is God challenging you this Advent to step out into a new part of your life or faith journey? What changes await you?

  _____

  _____

  _____

  _____

- Who are your companions on the journey? Have you played a key role in anyone else's journey?

_____

_____

_____

_____

Journaling space:

_____

_____

_____

_____

_____

_____

_____

_____

_____

_____

_____

_____

_____

In Thanksgiving

Thank you, Lord, for our companions.
Thank you for the people who walk with us.
When the road is long,
and the end is nowhere in sight,
teach us to lean on you,
and lean on each other,
as we step out into the unknown
for the hope of a better tomorrow.
In you we find our strength to carry on.
Walk with us today and always.
Amen.

Scripture: Second Reading

1 CORINTHIANS 1: 3-9 – CYCLE B

Grace to you and peace from God our Father and the Lord Jesus Christ. I give thanks to my God always on your account for the grace of God bestowed on you in Christ Jesus, that in him you were enriched in every way, with all discourse and all knowledge, as the testimony to Christ was confirmed among you, so that you are not lacking in any spiritual gift as you wait for the revelation of our Lord Jesus Christ. He will keep you firm to the end, irreproachable on the day of our Lord Jesus [Christ]. God is faithful, and by him you were called to fellowship with his Son, Jesus Christ our Lord.

Lectio Divina:

- Invite the Holy Spirit to be with you.
- **Lectio:** What word or phrase stands out?
- **Meditatio:** What is God saying to you today?
- **Oratio:** What do you have to say to God? How will your life change because of this passage?
- **Contemplatio:** thank God in silence.

Questions for Reflection:

- How were the early Christians different from us? How are we all the same?

  _____

  _____

  _____

  _____

- St. Paul says we all have spiritual gifts. Which gifts are you most blessed with? Which gifts do you need to nourish?

  _____

  _____

  _____

  _____

- St. Paul is grateful for the Church in Corinth. For whom are you most grateful?

_____

_____

_____

_____

Journaling space:

_____

_____

_____

_____

_____

_____

_____

_____

_____

_____

_____

_____

_____

_____

Mountains

The first mountain I ever climbed was the "tourist mountain" in Anchorage called Flattop.

Imagine this: two Indiana natives and one of my husband's military buddies (also from the lower 48) go to hike a mountain. It sounds like the setup to a joke, doesn't it? We were full of enthusiasm, but not forethought. It was 60 degrees and sunny in the Anchorage bowl, but freezing cold and blowing snow at the Flattop Trailhead.

We scrounged through the truck and found that we had one hat and one pair of gloves to share among the three of us, but we were not deterred. We were Alaskans now, darn it, and we were going to tackle this mountain if it was the last thing we did that day.

We followed the tracks of the hikers before us, through the slush and snow. The trail wound around through a treeline and up a steep, slippery slope, to the top, where the tracks before us ended.

It appeared to be aptly named: a large flat expanse of bare rock and snow, with gusts of wind that must have exceeded 50 miles an hour. We had bright red cheeks and potential for a trio of ear infections, but the feeling was exhilarating. Not a soul around, and here we are, screaming at the top of our lungs and laughing and celebrating our victory. Our very first mountain!

A month later, I became Youth Minister at a Catholic church in Anchorage. The first event I planned was the most Alaskan thing I could think of: a family hike on Flattop. A few people raised an eyebrow at the idea, but I assured them I'd done the hike once, and figured we would be back within a pair of hours.

We met at the trailhead and made our way to the top, up the same trail, now thawed after the last of the winter was gone. I hung back with the slowest of the group, and we made our way to that same flat mountaintop expanse that I'd climbed a month earlier. We were out of breath, but I was still full of exuberance. Everything was going so well.

Until I realized that none of my teenagers were there waiting for me.

I asked one of the students where everyone had gone. "We're hiking Flattop," she said, as if it was the most obvious thing in the world.

"So… where's Flattop?" I asked. An innocent question. She pointed: not one, but two peaks out, higher and deeper into the range, towering over us. An impossibility.

This is the part of the story where the Alaskans laugh at me. That little mountain we'd conquered on my first hike? It's called "Blueberry Hill." It's less than a third of the way up the full course of the trail.

Maybe your walk with Christ is a bit like my "mountaintop" experience. Maybe you're like me: doing the very best you can with what you have and what you know, but falling quite short of the mark. Our faith is so vast, like the national park systems, where Flattop is only one of a great many mountains.

How can I measure up to the great saints that went before me, much less my contemporaries, who seem to have it all together? They seem to pray with incredible fervor and love with their lives. I can't measure up to that. Except.

I am enough. I am a child of God.

My job is not to compete with the professionals who scale Denali, the tallest mountain in the northern hemisphere. My job is to give my best at hiking Flattop, and to rejoice in the little victories that are Blueberry Hill.

My job is to love the Lord in my littleness, to be his child, to delight in his creation and to share that joy with others. When God calls me higher, I will scale those mountains with all my strength and all my skill, not matter how little it may be. For now, the challenges he has placed in my life are more than enough.

I will climb each mountain. I will give my best for Christ, and he will give me the strength to carry on.

Questions for Reflection:

- What are the mountains that God has placed in your life?

_____

_____

_____

_____

- What parts of your life do you feel most equipped to handle? What parts make you feel out of your element?

_____

_____

_____

_____

- What are the little steps you can take today to help you reach the ultimate goal?

_____

_____

_____

_____

Journaling space:

_____

_____

_____

_____

_____

_____

_____

_____

_____

_____

_____

_____

_____

_____

_____

_____

_____

_____

Scripture: Gospel

MARK 13: 33-37 – CYCLE B

Be watchful! Be alert! You do not know when the time will come. It is like a man traveling abroad. He leaves home and places his servants in charge, each with his work, and orders the gatekeeper to be on the watch. Watch, therefore; you do not know when the lord of the house is coming, whether in the evening, or at midnight, or at cockcrow, or in the morning. May he not come suddenly and find you sleeping. What I say to you, I say to all: 'Watch!'"

Lectio Divina:

- Invite the Holy Spirit to be with you.
- **Lectio:** What word or phrase stands out?

- **Meditatio:** What is God saying to you today?
- **Oratio:** What do you have to say to God? How will your life change because of this passage?
- **Contemplatio:** thank God in silence.

Questions for Reflection:

- Which areas of your life are you most vigilant about?

_____

_____

_____

_____

- What does it mean to be watchful and alert in the context of faith?

- _____

_____

_____

_____

- How is God calling you to be more prepared?

_____

_____

Encounter:

_____

_____

Journaling space:

_____

_____

_____

_____

_____

_____

_____

_____

_____

_____

_____

_____

_____

_____

_____

_____

_____

_____

Waiting

My husband and I have a cat named Precious (yes, that's a Tolkien reference; bonus points to you if you get it). She's the easiest cat I've ever raised in my life. She knew how to use the litter box before we got her, she'll keep you company when you're bored, and she's quick to chase a piece of string. She's so mellow that we can roll her onto her back and play "pass the kitten:" sliding her back and forth across the kitchen tile floor without a fuss.

And then we got Achilles.

A Chesapeake Bay/Boxer mix, Achilles is another story altogether. His mother was a service dog, but his father was the neighbor dog who snuck under the fence, and thus, puppies. Achilles has the potential to be a smart dog, if he can mellow down enough to think before he acts.

Sit, shake, lay down: these were the basic tricks he learned as a puppy. Issues that are more problematic included a kennel and two adults who worked simultaneous day jobs. Suffice to say there were many tears from all parties involved, and frequent messes to clean up. We've thrown in the towel on carpeting; we'll replace it as soon as we have funds for a vinyl flooring. Some stains don't go away.

Despite the perils of raising a puppy, my husband and I did well. Of all the things Achilles learned, the best trick he knows is "wait."

We started him on it as soon as we got him, and for the most part, he's gotten quite good at it. Before every meal, he has to "sit," and then "wait" for as long as we decide. We fill the food and water bowl with the dog out of the way, and he descends upon the food with enthusiasm... only after we've released him.

Even harder "waits" involve playtime. We play fetch quite a bit, and sometimes we make him wait to retrieve the crown jewel of all dog toys: the tennis ball. We also practice "sit" and "wait" before we go... dare I say it out loud?... "outside" for a "walk."

Achilles would be good at Advent. He's used to "wait" over the past year we've had him. He knows that with a little patience and restraint, a great many good things will come to him.

As small children, we're taught the value of patience. Sometimes, even as adults, we need a refresher. Patience is delayed self-gratification, for the hope of a better tomorrow. That's Advent.

Christ has come to us, two thousand years ago, God made flesh, to be one with us. In one way, we are waiting for him as we prepare to celebrate Christmas. But in another sense, we are still waiting: we wait for his second coming.

Throughout Advent, and throughout our lifetimes, prepare our hearts for one of two outcomes. One options is that the end is near, as the doomsday folk say, and Christ's second coming into the world is right around the corner. The second option is that he will come to take us home at the end of our personal life, our earthly journey. Either way, we don't know how much time we have left, and our hearts must be ready.

Our waiting is different from the way my dog waits: Achilles's goal is to sit as still as possible and wait for as long as I tell him. His wait is one of inaction. Our goal, our wait, is the opposite: we work in our wait. We prepare our hearts, our lives, for the coming of our Lord. In fact, it's imperative that we not sit still and let our lives pass us by. We wait for Christ, yes, but in the meantime, we must live in a way that orients our hearts back to his own.

Today, let's practice patience as we wait for the coming of Christ. May our anticipation stir us to action. May he find us ready.

Questions for Reflection:

- Do you have any pets? What have they taught you over the years?

_____

_____

_____

_____

- What is the hardest part about waiting? Why do you find it so difficult?

  _____

  _____

  _____

  _____

- What are some concrete actions we can take towards Christ as we wait for his coming?

  _____

  _____

  _____

  _____

Week 1 Check-in

Congratulations! You've made it one week into Advent. I hope your time has been filled with hope. Take a minute to review some questions:

- Look back to your Pre-Advent Check-in (page 28). How well did you hold to your plans?

  _____

  _____

  _____

  _____

- What will you do differently this week?

  _____

  _____

_____

_____

- How did you give back to the community?

_____

_____

_____

_____

- What Advent traditions have you tried?

_____

_____

_____

_____

Before you go to Mass this week:
- Who/what will you pray for?

_____

_____

_____

_____

- Week 2 Homily Notes:

_____

_____

_____

_____

Journaling space:

_____

_____

_____

_____

_____

_____

_____

_____

_____

_____

_____

_____

_____

Week 2: Faith

Jesus, I trust in you.

I traveled to Krakow, Poland, for World Youth Day in the summer of 2016. I already had fallen in love with two great Polish saints, and this trip only solidified my love for them.

The first is Saint Faustina. I'd read her Diary during adoration in the months before the trip, and she amazed me by her simplicity and accessibility. Her writing was clear and straightforward, but beautiful and elegant. It was as if Jesus spoke to me as he spoke to her. The Chaplet of Divine Mercy had been a part of our family prayer growing up, but it became a theme in my life: Jesus, I trust in you. In every adversity, in every struggle: Jesus, I trust in you.

The second great Polish saint is Pope Saint John Paul II. I felt a kinship to him and his love for the land, for his community, for the arts and the church. He was so grounded, so humble, and yet he loved with his whole heart and wasn't afraid to stand up for what was right. His words, too, have continued to give me courage: Be not afraid. I began to think of him as an adopted grandfather as I walked through his home in Wadowice. He is still with me, encouraging me to trust: be not afraid.

There are many layers to hope. Sometimes our lives can be so overwhelming, and we aren't sure if we'll make it through this part of our lives. The deeper we look, the more we realize how small we are in the grand scheme of things. God is in control. He is larger, greater, stronger than we can imagine. But his size and his strength don't diminish his love and care for each one of us. It's one thing to believe in God's word, and another thing altogether to learn to trust him and be in relationship with him.

Our hope for a better day, a better life, an eternity of happiness, stems from the faith that God is good and he has our best interests at heart. It is difficult to surrender to God and place our trust in him, but it is a critical part on the journey to Christ.

This week, surrender to him. Trust in him. Have faith. He makes all things new.

Questions for Reflection:

- Which saints are your favorites? Why do you relate to them?

  _____

  _____

  _____

  _____

- Do you find it difficult to surrender to God's will and place your trust in him? If so, what is holding you back?

  _____

  _____

  _____

  _____

- What words or prayers of hope keep you grounded in times of trouble? Write them here, and take them to heart.

  _____

  _____

  _____

  _____

Prayer of Surrender

Jesus,
I know you are in control.
I know you have my best interests in mind.
It's still hard, letting you lead the way.
Teach me to have faith in your goodness.
Help me to fight for justice,
and to rely on your providence,
trusting that you will take care of the rest
when I've done all I can do.
I trust in you.
Amen.

Scripture: First Reading

ISAIAH 40: 1-5, 9-11 – CYCLE B

Comfort, give comfort to my people, says your God. Speak to the heart of Jerusalem, and proclaim to her that her service has ended, that her guilt is expiated, that she has received from the hand of the LORD double for all her sins. A voice proclaims: In the wilderness prepare the way of the LORD! Make straight in the wasteland a highway for our God! Every valley shall be lifted up, every mountain and hill made low; the rugged land shall be a plain, the rough country, a broad valley. Then the glory of the LORD shall be revealed, and all flesh shall see it together; for the mouth of the LORD has spoken. Go up onto a high mountain, Zion, herald of good news! Cry out at the top of your voice, Jerusalem, herald of good news! Cry out, do not fear! Say to the cities of Judah: Here is your God! Here comes with power the Lord GOD, who rules by his strong arm; here is his reward with him, his recompense before him. Like a shepherd he feeds his flock; in his arms he gathers the lambs, carrying them in his bosom, leading the ewes with care.

Lectio Divina:

- Invite the Holy Spirit to be with you.
- **Lectio:** What word or phrase stands out?
- **Meditatio:** What is God saying to you today?
- **Oratio:** What do you have to say to God? How will your life change because of this passage?
- **Contemplatio:** thank God in silence.

Questions for Reflection:

- Where is God granting you comfort?

  _____

  _____

  _____

  _____

- God works mighty deeds, and carries us in his arms like lambs. Which God do you relate to

most: a God of tenderness, or a God of might?
Or somewhere in between?

_____

_____

_____

_____

- How are you preparing the way of the Lord?
  How can we shout from the mountaintops in
  today's modern society?

_____

_____

_____

_____

Journaling space:

_____

_____

_____

_____

_____

_____

_____

Luggage

Oh, luggage. How mysterious are your ways.

It's always the same: as I pack my bags for a trip, everything fits. Period. The space is well used, and sometimes I even leave some extra space for the return trip. Souvenirs and other items.

No matter how much forethought I put into packing, it doesn't matter: nothing will ever fit so well again. After day one my travels, I'm left scratching my head at how impossible it is to make everything fit into the bags I brought with me.

My personality is a part of the problem, to be honest. I'm always trying to think ahead and prepare for the unexpected. Translated to packing, that means six extra pairs of socks and baby powder and two extra jackets and hiking boots. In my mind, I'm ready for anything.

If I'm flying or traveling by some other form of public transportation, there's the question of the carry-on (not to mention the restrictions surrounding baggage for airlines!). The carry-on is the ultimate preparedness challenge: if the rest of my luggage gets lost, can I survive on everything inside this backpack? My apocalyptic mindset goes haywire, and surprise, this bag contains double of everything. And God forbid I should forget my phone charger!

Because I want to be prepared.

I got smart a few years back and created a "toiletries bag" full of all the bathroom and medical essentials: soap, shampoo, meds... you name it, I have it. Probably. It's the first thing I pack when I prepare to travel. It makes me feel ready.

As important as all this packing is, and as perfect as I try to make it be, it's never enough. I always forget something, or encounter an emergency need that requires a run to the store. Yet, as reflect on my past adventures, I realize I've never gone without. I've never been in a place where I couldn't escape my inconvenience with the help of my wallet and a trip to the store.

I wish I had the faith to match my God's awesome providence.

Jesus tells us in the Gospels not to pack for the journey (Luke 9:3). He tells us that he clothes the lilies of the fields, and gives the sparrows homes (Matthew 6: 25-

34). If God cares for plants and animals, he will take care of his sons and daughters, too.

God will provide for all my needs. It's time I trust him to do that.

It's time to leave behind some of the extra baggage I've been carrying around with me: for better, or for worse. We each carry emotional baggage, regrets, guilt, painful memories. We pack them down and wrap them up until we almost forget we're carrying them, but they're still there. All that baggage- it's dead weight. No matter how much we rationalize it, these things will never save us or help us out. It's holding us back from a better life, from freedom.

This Advent, let's cut out some dead weight in our baggage. Let's clear the space to make room for Jesus. Let's trust that we are in the hands of a capable Creator, who knows what we need even before we ask.

When I travel to visit family this Christmas, I'll be packing light. I'll leave the rest up to him.

Questions for Reflection:

- What's one thing you never leave home without? What's another thing you always over-pack?

_____

_____

_____

_____

- What's holding you back from trusting in God's providence?

  _____

  _____

  _____

  _____

- What kinds of negative baggage are you holding onto? Can you find the courage to leave it behind?

  _____

  _____

  _____

  _____

Journaling space:

_____

_____

_____

_____

_____

_____

Prayer for Encouragement

Lord,

Sometimes, life is an uphill battle.

It's all I can do to make it through another day.

I feel weighed down by all these burdens.

I know you will give me strength,

But it just doesn't *feel* enough.

Help me to reach out when I need help.

Grant me courage, resiliency, patience.

Show me which burdens I must carry,

and which burdens are meant for your shoulders.

And help me trust in your strength

to carry me through this storm.

You are my God.

You are enough.

Amen.

Scripture: Second Reading

2 PETER 3: 8-14 – CYCLE B

But do not ignore this one fact, beloved, that with the Lord one day is like a thousand years and a thousand years like one day. The Lord does not delay his promise, as some regard "delay," but he is patient with you, not wishing that any should perish but that all should come to repentance. But the day of the Lord will come like a thief, and then the heavens will pass away with a mighty roar and the elements will be dissolved by fire, and the earth and everything done on it will be found out. Since everything is to be dissolved in this way, what sort of persons ought [you] to be, conducting yourselves in holiness and devotion, waiting for and hastening the coming of the day of God, because of which the heavens will be dissolved in flames and the elements melted by fire. But according to his promise we await new heavens and a new earth in which righteousness dwells. Therefore, beloved, since you await these things, be eager to be found without spot or blemish before him, at peace.

Lectio Divina:

- Invite the Holy Spirit to be with you.
- **Lectio:** What word or phrase stands out?
- **Meditatio:** What is God saying to you today?
- **Oratio:** What do you have to say to God? How will your life change because of this passage?
- **Contemplatio:** thank God in silence.

Questions for Reflection:

- How has God been patient with you?

_____

_____

_____

_____

- How is God challenging you to prepare yourself for his coming? What actions can you take today?

_____

_____

_____

_____

- Where is God calling you to repentance?

_____

_____

_____

_____

Journaling space:

_____

_____

_____

_____

_____

_____

_____

_____

_____

_____

Pathways

"Don't we turn right here?"

"Nope. Definitely left."

"Are you sure? I think we passed it. Isn't it back that way?"

"Keep going. You'll see here in a minute."

So go the conversations between my husband and I when one of us is driving in unfamiliar territory. I get lost driving on base, with all the parking lots and buildings with numbers and acronyms instead of words or phrases. For him, it's south Anchorage. I know the area pretty well because I work in the area, and he second-guesses my fastest routes.

Although I'd consider myself a generally optimistic and inclusive person, I realize I can be more than a little hardheaded. When I know I'm right, I'll go to lengths to get my way, even if it means a little conflict. That's saying something, because most people know that I'm a committed conflict-avoidant personality.

The perfect storm happens when we're both earning a new area together. When we're going to a new place, one of us will navigate with a GPS on a phone, and the other will drive. I'd like to say that I'm the better navigator, but I know he'll disagree, so suffice to say that we both have our moments.

Of course, road signs are hard to see (especially when it's night), and then there's a detour or road closure. At that point, both our strong personalities come out. The GPS is demanding one thing while the navigator tries to figure out which road is which. Then we're in the wrong lane because of traffic, and we're late, and flustered, and end up taking the long way around.

John the Baptist calls for us to prepare the way of the Lord and to make straight his paths. That's a nice picture, isn't it? Straight roads with well-lit signage and plenty of median and shoulder. In a perfect world, our paths would be straight as interstates. Each person would look out for the needs of his or her neighbors, and work to serve each other.

But the reality is different. Interstates are a nice idea, but they steal people's property and homes, and divert us around neighborhoods with real people and real lives. Interstates aren't always realistic. Sometimes they're downright impossible. Sometimes we have to take the long way, the slow way. God works through the detours, the slow-downs, the turnouts.

I get caught up in the little details of life and want to do everything, exactly so, by myself, the way I want it. Part of it is creativity, part of it is control, but a good chunk of it is stubbornness. I want things the way I want them, darn it. But we're not called to convenience. To make straight the Lord's path, we have to get our hands dirty.

As is the case with anyone going through transitions, it's easy to get overwhelmed by the number of paths to choose. There are so many good things, and so many easy things, to choose. How do we know where God calls us? Through prayer, and patience, and listening... but ultimately, with a step of faith.

God has the best plans in mind for us, and while we cooperate in the act of finding our way, we can find comfort knowing he will lead us along the right road.

Questions for Reflection:

- How good are you at following directions- literally and metaphorically?

_____

_____

_____

_____

- Does God want your life to be like an interstate, or like a back road? In what ways?

  _____

  _____

  _____

  _____

- When will you have time this week to slow down and spend some time listening to the Lord and what he wants your path to look like? Schedule it in, so you don't miss it.

  _____

  _____

  _____

  _____

Journaling space:

_____

_____

_____

_____

_____

_____

_____

_____

Pathways Prayer

Lord, I know you have a plan for my life.
I know I need to hear your voice.
Speak to me today.
Help me to open my heart to hear your voice.
Guide me on right paths.
Bend my will to yours,
so I may serve you in everything I do.
Amen.

Scripture: Gospel

MARK 1: 1-8 – CYCLE B

The beginning of the gospel of Jesus Christ
[the Son of God]. As it is written in Isaiah the
prophet: "Behold, I am sending my messenger
ahead of you; he will prepare your way. A voice of
one crying out in the desert: 'Prepare the way of
the Lord, make straight his paths.'" John [the]
Baptist appeared in the desert proclaiming a
baptism of repentance for the forgiveness of sins.
People of the whole Judean countryside and all the
inhabitants of Jerusalem were going out to him
and were being baptized by him in the Jordan River
as they acknowledged their sins. John was clothed
in camel's hair, with a leather belt around his
waist. He fed on locusts and wild honey. And this
is what he proclaimed: "One mightier than I is

> coming after me. I am not worthy to stoop and loosen the thongs of his sandals. I have baptized you with water; he will baptize you with the holy Spirit."

Lectio Divina:

- Invite the Holy Spirit to be with you.
- **Lectio:** What word or phrase stands out?
- **Meditatio:** What is God saying to you today?
- **Oratio:** What do you have to say to God? How will your life change because of this passage?
- **Contemplatio:** thank God in silence.

Questions for Reflection:

- How can you be like John the Baptist today?

  _____

  _____

  _____

  _____

- How has your baptism changed your life?

  _____

  _____

  _____

  _____

- When was the last time you received the sacrament of Reconciliation? If it has been a while, what's holding you back? Make a commitment to receive the sacrament sometime during Advent before Christmas.

_____

_____

_____

_____

Journaling space:

_____

_____

_____

_____

_____

_____

_____

_____

_____

_____

_____

Opposites

My husband and I are polar opposites of each other. It's equal parts endearing and maddening.

He's tall (over six feet), and I'm short (not much above five feet). He loves to go to the gym and I love arts and crafts, though we'll both make exceptions from time to time. He abhors making small talk and I want to stay and chat with half the congregation after every Mass. He is straightforward in word and action, while I bend over backwards to accommodate someone, despite my misgivings.

One of my favorite pictures of us is from his home back in Indiana. We were clearing some of the woods, and he's carrying a log across his shoulders, his face all red from the effort, and I'm holding... a stick. It's an accurate portrayal of us: sometimes our differences are annoying, and sometimes they're hilarious.

Because we're so different, we disagree on a whole variety of topics. We get into silly arguments about things like words (how do you pronounce the word "dull?") and proper ways to load the silverware in the dishwasher. Often, after a few back-and-forth arguments, we realize we'd agreed all along, and were talking from two different viewpoints.

After one such disagreement-turned-agreement, I said in exasperation, "We disagree on everything, don't we?"

You know what he said? "No, we don't."

I couldn't have said it better myself.

The one thing that we always agree on is our faith. I may lean towards a pastoral standpoint while he favors strict orthodoxy, but we are both committed to our Catholic identity. Even if we worship in different ways and have different images of God, we always worship together at Mass.

After the context of our faith, our differences seem to balance each other out. He demands that I stand up for myself, and I soften his rough edges. It's a good trade.

The Church's teachings seem counter-intuitive to our expectations, especially in light of society's standards. Words like judgment, freedom, and justice appear to have a different meaning in light of God's message. But the deeper we dig into our faith, the more we realize that God's Word is liberating, not confining, and that we have agreed all along.

Questions for Reflection:

- Do you have a family member or friend who is your polar opposite? Or someone who thinks and acts exactly like you do? What balances things out?

  _____

  _____

  _____

  _____

- Where are you standing opposite God this Advent? What brings about such opposition? What do you need to bring things together?

  _____

  _____

  _____

  _____

- How can we begin to soften our hearts and reconcile with one another?

  _____

  _____

  _____

  _____

Week 2 Check-in

You're another week into Advent. Tomorrow is the halfway point, and our faith will turn to joy. Take a minute to review some questions:

- Look back to your Week One Check-in (page 59). How well did you hold to your plans?

  _____

  _____

  _____

  _____

- What will you do differently this week?

  _____

  _____

_____

_____

- How did you give back to the community?

_____

_____

_____

_____

- What Advent traditions have tried?

_____

_____

_____

_____

Before you go to Mass this week:
- Who/what will you pray for?

_____

_____

_____

_____

- Week 3 Homily Notes:

Encounter:

_____

_____

_____

_____

Journaling space:

_____

_____

_____

_____

_____

_____

_____

_____

_____

_____

_____

_____

_____

_____

_____

_____

Week 3: Joy

When we were growing up, we'd stop by two houses to every Christmas. I don't think my parents knew the people who lived there, or if they did, we didn't know them well enough to visit any other time of the year. The real reason we stopped by were the fantastic Christmas light displays.

There weren't mere lights hung from the roof and windows of the house. That's the stuff of amateurs. These two houses had it going on. There were inflatable decorations, two-dimensional outlined caricatures, a glowing plastic nativity, an arc of reindeer... you name it, they had it. The whole street was lit up and flashing Christmas from the zealous decorations.

Keep in mind that these two houses were on the same side of the street. One was a corner lot, which I always thought had the unfair advantage, because they had a lot more yard space. To my amusement, a single house stood between the two light-houses. Guess how many decorations were on that house. That's right. Zero. Not so much as a tree in the front window or a strand of lights on the porch.

Every year, we would visit that street for an ultra-slow drive by. We probably even put it in park, when my sisters were younger. I remember looking out the window of the van and marveling at all the colors. There were so many things to look at; I felt like I had to notice all the details, and fast, before we rolled away. It took a solid minute to note each item in the yards, placed, hung, and lit, with so much care.

These women (I imagine them as cute little old ladies, anyway) understood the wonder of Christmas. The dancing lights are one of the most fundamental components of American Christmas decorations. We become like children again, celebrating the little things. Our hearts are aglow with the beauty and wonder of it all.

I hope I lead my life like one of the Christmas-houses, not like the poor family that lived in the middle of it all. I want my light to shine. I want my home to glow. Because that's what faith is all about, isn't it?

Faith should be less of a spotlight, shining with a harsh, stringent beam... and more like a candle, or a Christmas light. We are not called to point out all the glaring errors in someone's life. We must start with a warmth, a sense of belonging and love, a promise of acceptance. We must first have faith in the lost, and show them that we care, before they will come to have faith in our Lord.

This Advent, as we prepare our hearts and homes for Christmas, may we all return to the simple joys and wonders of Christmas. May we be the warm light for the lost. Together, let's marvel at the beauty of the colors, the warmth of family, and the reason for the season.

Questions for Reflection:

- Do you err to the side of over-decorating or under-decorating for Christmas?

  _____

  _____

  _____

  _____

- What are some of your favorite Advent/Christmas seasons that bring joy to your life?

  _____

  _____

  _____

  _____

- What are some ways you can let your light of faith be a glow of warmth to others this Advent?

_____

_____

_____

_____

Journaling space:

In Thanksgiving for the Little Things
Thank you, God,
for all the goodness you give us each Christmas season.
Thank you for the food we share with family and friends.
Thank you for the songs of joyful celebration.
Thank you for the laughter of children,
who remind us to celebrate life and simplicity.
Grant us childlike faith,
that we may love unconditionally
and run to you with open arms.
Amen.

Scripture: First Reading

ISAIAH 61: 1-2A, 10-11 – CYCLE B

The spirit of the Lord GOD is upon me, because the LORD has anointed me; He has sent me to bring good news to the afflicted, to bind up the brokenhearted, to proclaim liberty to the captives, release to the prisoners, to announce a year of favor from the LORD and a day of vindication by our God; I will rejoice heartily in the LORD, my being exults in my God; for he has clothed me with garments of salvation, and wrapped me in a robe of justice, like a bridegroom adorned with a diadem, as a bride adorns herself with her jewels. As the earth brings forth its shoots, and a garden makes its seeds spring up, so will the Lord GOD make justice spring up, and praise before all the nations.

Lectio Divina:

- Invite the Holy Spirit to be with you.
- **Lectio:** What word or phrase stands out?
- **Meditatio:** What is God saying to you today?
- **Oratio:** What do you have to say to God? How will your life change because of this passage?
- **Contemplatio:** thank God in silence.

Questions for Reflection:

- Of all the people God calls us to reach out to, which people do you relate to most easily? Who is a challenge for you?

_____

_____

_____

_____

- We are anointed with holy oil during some of the sacraments. Which anointings have you received?

_____

_____

_____

_____

- How has God blessed you this Advent season?

_____

_____

_____

_____

Journaling space:

_____

_____

_____

_____

_____

_____

_____

_____

_____

_____

_____

_____

_____

Guests

I have a theory that every family has the same secret: our homes are messy when there are no guests.

Granted, when I go over to someone's house, I am the guest, so I haven't been able to verify my theory. Or it could be a way to make me feel better about the chaos that is our home when no one is coming over.

Something about people coming over to the house makes us re-evaluate the state of things. The socks and shoes scattered across the floor become noticeable. The dishes in the sink are a scourge to humanity, and the household chooses one room to be the "dump stuff here until the guests leave" room.

I remember having guests over as a child: energized with the threat of "they'll be here in twenty minutes! Put this pile of stuff in your bedroom." Then there's the wiping down of all the surfaces and setting the table for the guests. The ritual happens with all guests, even relatives, who already know you and can't disown you over the bookshelf that you've never dusted.

There's this strange instinct to put on a show for someone who's coming over. We want to put our best foot forward—doubly so if it's someone we are getting to know for the first time. Add the frantic "clean the house" mentality to the stress of accommodating large groups of people, and meal preparation. Thus, we have a recipe for holidays, dreaded as a time of work and exhaustion instead of a time of relaxation and community.

We've all heard this "cleaning house" metaphor when it comes to "preparing our hearts for Jesus." But preparing our hearts for Jesus is different from cleaning house in a few ways. First, he knows the stuff we have in our houses, and we can't hide the dirty laundry behind the closed door of the spare bedroom. There's no fooling this guy.

Second, Jesus doesn't want us to try to fool him. He doesn't want us to bury all our secrets and family dirt in the dark. He wants to clean us, heal us, and make us whole, happy, holy people. It doesn't get much better than that.

Even when our houses and our hearts are a mess, and we're having a hard time finding the time, space, and courage to clean things up, Jesus loves us anyway. He comes to us anyway. He's the best friend, not the random acquaintance, who has seen it all, and is not deterred. He is here to help. Open the door and let him in.

Questions for Reflection:

- What are your top priorities of housekeeping before the holiday hits?

  _____

  _____

  _____

  _____

- What bits of dust and dirt need cleaning in your life, in order to make room for Jesus?

  _____

  _____

  _____

  _____

- How will you ask Jesus for help in preparing your heart and your home for Christmas?

  _____

  _____

  _____

  _____

Scripture: Second Reading

1 THESSALONIANS 5: 16-24 – CYCLE B

Rejoice always. Pray without ceasing. In all circumstances give thanks, for this is the will of God for you in Christ Jesus. Do not quench the Spirit. Do not despise prophetic utterances. Test everything; retain what is good. Refrain from every kind of evil. May the God of peace himself make you perfectly holy and may you entirely, spirit, soul, and body, be preserved blameless for the coming of our Lord Jesus Christ. The one who calls you is faithful, and he will also accomplish it.

Lectio Divina:

- Invite the Holy Spirit to be with you.
- **Lectio:** What word or phrase stands out?

- **Meditatio:** What is God saying to you today?
- **Oratio:** What do you have to say to God? How will your life change because of this passage?
- **Contemplatio:** thank God in silence.

Questions for Reflection:

- Which of these little faith tips stood out to you most? Why do you think it stood out to you?

  _____

  _____

  _____

  _____

- How have you seen God acting in your life to make you holy?

  _____

  _____

  _____

  _____

- What are you thankful for? What causes you to rejoice?

  _____

  _____

"They don't have to be fancy gifts, right?" I reasoned. We realized she didn't want all the fancy gifts that money could buy, but she did appreciate little gifts, especially the crafty ones made by hand.

Growing up, we didn't buy things for each other for birthdays or the holidays. We still don't spend much money on presents. Our currency is creativity: blankets and quilts, handmade cards and stuffed animals, decorations and trinkets. Our family's collective love language is creativity.

By the third week of Advent, unless your super-organized and prepared (I'm neither of those things, most days), we're still picking up last-minute Christmas presents. If you're like my family, you're spending every waking minute trying to finish a project that became bigger than you initially intended.

So, as you're shopping for gifts, consider this: what are you getting Jesus for his birthday?

A better question yet is this one: what do you think Jesus wants most from you for his birthday? An easy, sappy answer might be "my heart," or "return to the faith," or "giving up a particular vice." But resist the urge to think superficial, and dig deeper: what does Jesus want for his birthday? And parallel to that question: what do you have that you can give him? If one of Jesus's love languages is gifts, what could you give him this Christmas?

It reminds me of the parable of the talents. We each have a specific talent; how are we using them to multiply and grow our gifts? Like the story of the Little Drummer Boy, we can give baby Jesus whatever talent or gift we have, no matter how small or unconventional. That's the best gift we can give to our Lord: the surplus from the talents he first gave us.

This Advent, think about what you can give- or continue to give- to Jesus. Be creative. Our Lord delights in us. He won't be disappointed.

Questions for Reflection:

- What is the best gift you've ever received for Christmas? What was the best gift you've ever given someone?

_____

_____

_____

_____

- What will you give Jesus for Christmas this year? What do you need to do to get this gift ready?

_____

_____

_____

_____

- How will you speak a language of love to those in your life this Advent?

_____

_____

_____

_____

Journaling space:

A Prayer of Joy

God,
you never cease to amaze me.
I am so blessed to be a part of your family,
your beloved child.
You have made me a new creation,
free to worship you, to love you, to serve you.
Fill my heart with joy in these days of preparation.
Guide me in your footsteps.
Let my life be a light to the world,
bringing the lost back home to your loving arms.
I am so blessed to be a part of your mission.
May my life give you glory.
Amen.

Scripture: Gospel

JOHN 1: 6-8, 19-28 – CYCLE B

A man named John was sent from God. He came for testimony, to testify to the light, so that all might believe through him. He was not the light, but came to testify to the light. And this is the testimony of John. When the Jews from Jerusalem sent priests and Levites [to him] to ask him, "Who are you?" he admitted and did not deny it, but admitted, "I am not the Messiah." So they asked him, "What are you then? Are you Elijah?" And he said, "I am not." "Are you the Prophet?" He answered, "No." So they said to him, "Who are you, so we can give an answer to those who sent us? What do you have to say for yourself?" He said: "I am 'the voice of one crying out in the desert, "Make straight the way of the Lord,"'" as

Isaiah the prophet said." Some Pharisees were also sent. They asked him, "Why then do you baptize if you are not the Messiah or Elijah or the Prophet?" John answered them, "I baptize with water; but there is one among you whom you do not recognize, the one who is coming after me, whose sandal strap I am not worthy to untie." This happened in Bethany across the Jordan, where John was baptizing.

Lectio Divina:

- Invite the Holy Spirit to be with you.
- **Lectio:** What word or phrase stands out?
- **Meditatio:** What is God saying to you today?
- **Oratio:** What do you have to say to God? How will your life change because of this passage?
- **Contemplatio:** thank God in silence.

Questions for Reflection:

- How are you the light for people around you?

_____

_____

_____

_____

- If someone called you a Christian, what proof is there in your life of that fact?

_____

_____

_____

_____

- How can you prepare the way for Jesus, and for the next generation?

_____

_____

_____

_____

Journaling space:

_____

_____

_____

_____

_____

_____

_____

_____

Countdown

The role of Youth Minister is part faith formation, part community building, and part event organizer.

My husband asked me one day what I did at work every day. Do I need to be at work, if I don't have a youth night, or one-on-one meeting, or upcoming retreat? The answer? Yes, I need to go to work. I have to plan stuff.

Youth Ministry should be a triple-major: theology, education, and business. I have the theology part, and I have pieces of the education part, but my business side is a different challenge altogether.

They don't teach you in theology class how to write a budget, or plan a semester, or create advertising material.

Even beyond Youth Ministry, I imagine most event organizers share the same struggle: the notorious deadline. Translation: you will receive the great bulk of your registrations within 48 hours of this mark. Plan accordingly.

This is always the case in Youth Ministry, at least, for me. Of the 10 kids who sign up for the next RSVP-related event, eight of them will submit their online forms at 10:00pm on the day of the deadline.

Even in my personal life, there's always a running clock in the back of my mind. I have a few days left to finish this task. A few hours left before this meeting begins. A few minutes until the timer goes off and supper is ready. We're always glancing at a clock and judging timelines.

Procrastination is a professional skill that goes hand-in-hand with deadlines. How close I can get to the deadline before I need to kick it in and get things moving, to slide under the deadline at the last possible second?

Time is a great motivator: it's a push that gets us moving in the right direction, to land at the proper destination at the proper time. We all take that little push from the clock: time's almost here! Get a move on!

I've never used one of those chocolate countdown Advent calendars, and for good reason: nobody needs a couple dozen extra pieces of candy in a sugar-saturated season. We had a few different Advent calendars in my childhood. I remember the kind with doors that opened to pictures, or sticky pieces that attached to certain spots on a giant foam tree.

Advent calendars are the time marker that tracks our progress as we get us closer and closer to the final event: Christmas is almost here!

Week 3 of Advent is exactly that: Jesus is coming! We will not find a greater joy in all the earth. The season of Advent is not designed to make us panic that the deadline is coming up. It's to ease us into the reality that one of the biggest moments in salvation history is approaching. Salvation is a good thing! Don't panic; be joyful!

Advent is less of a frantic countdown to when a paper is due and more of a New Year's Eve countdown. We celebrate this season with joyful preparation: something greater than a new year is coming. It's the opportunity for a new life.

This Advent, rather than being swept up into last minute panicked deadlines, I hope I'm taking some time for what's important. Faith, family, friends. May the joy and peace of Christ be with you as you continue preparing your hearts and your homes for the season.

Questions for Reflection:

- What are you anticipating most about this upcoming Christmas season? What is most stressful about the upcoming season?

_____

_____

_____

_____

- What are you putting off in preparing, spiritually speaking? Why are you procrastinating?

  _____

  _____

  _____

  _____

- What can you to make this a joyful Christmas season? How can you keep it a priority, instead of being lost in the shuffle?

  _____

  _____

  _____

  _____

Journaling space:

_____

_____

_____

_____

_____

_____

Week 3 Check-in

One more week before Christmas! You're almost there! Take a minute to review some questions:

- Look back to your Week 2 Check-in (page 88). How well did you hold to your plans?

  _____

  _____

  _____

  _____

- What will you do differently this week?

  _____

  _____

_____

_____

- How did you give back to the community?

_____

_____

_____

_____

- What Advent traditions have you tried?

_____

_____

_____

_____

Before you go to Mass this week:
- Who/what will you pray for?

_____

_____

_____

_____

- Week 4 Homily Notes:

- _____

_____

_____

_____

Journaling space:

_____

_____

_____

_____

_____

_____

_____

_____

_____

_____

_____

_____

_____

_____

_____

Week 4: Peace

Before my husband and I got married, we did a Marian Consecration together. I still have the original book, with the dates and signatures in the back from our first Consecration. We would meet after classes when we could (as he went to college in Indianapolis, too), and read the book together in his truck, or my room, or the chapel. We made our consecration at the chapel at Marian University in Indianapolis, my alma mater. We did a second consecration again on the day of our wedding. Mary and Joseph have always been role models in our relationship.

Mary has been the model of Christian life for men and women alike for millennia. Her "yes" to God during this Sunday's Gospel (see page 138) is one that we all strive to emulate. Every Christian is called to Mary's level of purity, simplicity, and devotion.

Religious artwork often shows Mary as a thin, angelic, beautiful young woman, but it would be a mistake to think that Mary's goodness makes her weak. In fact, if we know anything about Mary, it is that her courage in the face of adversity is what makes her stand apart. She had every right to be afraid, from the time of Gabriel's annunciation through her son's death on the cross. And yet, she trusted that God would do as he said. She was resilient. That's something that can't be portrayed in a painting.

We would be remiss to reflect on Joseph's role in this situation, too. He could have condemned Mary or made her a public spectacle. By Jewish law, he could have had her killed. But he is an honorable man and chooses to uphold her dignity, even in the face of what must have been an incredible amount of pain. When God speaks to him in a dream and gives him courage, he acts, and without hesitation (Matthew 1:18-25). I want my "Yes" to be as great as Mary's, and I admire the great courage it took for Joseph to make his "Yes" to God, too.

Just as Mary is the ideal role model for mothers and wives, Joseph is the ideal role model for fathers and husbands. Joseph's life- the few details we know about him- make him a role model for soldiers, too. Joseph was a carpenter, so he must have been strong. He was obedient to God's will, and protected his wife and child from those who meant to harm them. Although he never speaks in any of the Gospels, his mere presence is a rock, a surety, a comfort. Joseph's life and actions make him the perfect role model for our military personnel.

Mary's Magnificat (Luke 1: 46-55) is a second example of our call as Christians: to say yes to God in all things, and to "magnify" him. May God be the greatest focus of our lives, and may we celebrate the fulfillment of all the Lord's promises through Jesus.

Like Mary, we ponder all these things in our hearts this Advent. We turn our hearts to God and rejoice with her always, surrendering our lives to God's will. Like Joseph, we hold fast to what is right and are a rock of refuge to our loved ones.

A practical note on the fourth week of Advent: it rarely lasts a full week. I've provided the full week's reflections, even though the Fourth Week of Advent 2017 falls on a Sunday, with Christmas day the following Monday. Use the rest of the reflections to round out your Christmas season, if you don't have a Christmas guidebook planned.

Questions for Reflection:

- Which of Mary and Joseph's qualities most inspires you? Which quality do you wish to emulate more fully?

_____

_____

_____

_____

- What progress have you made so far this Advent? What do you hope to gain as you continue your walk with the Lord?

  _____

  _____

  _____

  _____

- What is holding you back from making God the first and most important person in your life?

  _____

  _____

  _____

  _____

Journaling space:

_____

_____

_____

_____

_____

Scripture: First Reading

2 SAMUEL 7: 1-5, 8B-12, 14A, 16 – CYCLE B

After the king had taken up residence in his house, and the LORD had given him rest from his enemies on every side, the king said to Nathan the prophet, "Here I am living in a house of cedar, but the ark of God dwells in a tent!" Nathan answered the king, "Whatever is in your heart, go and do, for the LORD is with you." But that same night the word of the LORD came to Nathan: Go and tell David my servant, Thus says the LORD: Is it you who would build me a house to dwell in? I took you from the pasture, from following the flock, to become ruler over my people Israel. I was with you wherever you went, and I cut down all your enemies before you. And I will make your name like that of the greatest on earth. I will assign a place for my people Israel and I will plant them in it to dwell there; they will never again be disturbed, nor shall the wicked ever again oppress them, as they did at the beginning, and from the day when I appointed judges over my people Israel. I will give you rest from all your enemies. Moreover, the LORD also declares to you that the LORD will make a house for you: when your days have been completed and you rest with your ancestors, I will raise up your offspring after you, sprung from your loins, and I will establish his kingdom. I will be a father to him, and he shall be a son to me. Your house and your kingdom are firm forever before me; your throne shall be firmly established forever.

Lectio Divina:

- Invite the Holy Spirit to be with you.
- **Lectio:** What word or phrase stands out?
- **Meditatio:** What is God saying to you today?
- **Oratio:** What do you have to say to God? How will your life change because of this passage?
- **Contemplatio:** thank God in silence.

Questions for Reflection:

- Where does God dwell in your life? How can you make your heart a home for him?

_____

_____

_____

_____

- How has God been a companion and protector to you?

  _____

  _____

  _____

  _____

- How does your family put God first in your life? How is faith a part of your family traditions?

  _____

  _____

  _____

  _____

Journaling space:

_____

_____

_____

Emmanuel

God is with us.

I never understood what that meant until a retreat when I was in 6th grade.

Up until that point, church was a social community, an obligation, but not a relationship. I had been in Catholic school for my entire elementary school life, and I grew up in a vibrant, connected Catholic community. I didn't know a single Protestant until I went to middle school. I remember being surprised that my new public school friends didn't all go to Catholic school, too.

All this, and yet, I didn't know Jesus on a relational level until 6th grade. That's something you can't teach. It's someone you have to encounter: through his grace, not by any merit on my part.

On a diocesan retreat I attended, we experienced an adoration procession. Jesus came to each of us, individually, and I remember the girl I came with- the only other young person I knew in the room- was crying. I realized then that this Jesus- the one I knew all these facts about- was here. In this room. In front of me. He was with us, present in the Eucharist.

And even more, he wanted a relationship with me.

My faith changed that night. Up until that moment, I had been an "academic Catholic." I knew everything about Jesus, but I never knew Jesus. For most of us, this is how we start out. We learn the basics of Christianity: Jesus lived a long time ago, he loves you, and here are several stories about him.

But there comes a critical moment, a tipping point, where faith has to go deeper. We have to come to know the real, living God. Christ is more than rules and parables. Our Savior died for love of the individual, not the masses. And that love is still here, today, and still just as personal.

My faith began through community, and has grown to maturity through the sacraments. It began with Baptism, and continues with Confirmation and Matrimony, but doesn't stop there. Faith is a growth process: we have to keep going. I build my relationship with Jesus through the Eucharist and Reconciliation, where I encounter his presence and mercy. God is always there, but not in a passive sense. God acts in our lives. The more I get to know him, the more I appreciate his sense of humor. He is full of surprises. Sometimes, I have to sit there, shake my head, and laugh at the cleverness of God's works.

One of my favorite quotes says it like this: God always answers our prayers. He'll say one of three things:

- Yes.
- Not yet.
- I have something better in mind.

God is with each one of us, and seeking a relationship. Today, let's open our hearts: not for words or teaching, but for love. When Love comes in, and makes a home in our lives, then the peace of Christ will fill our hearts and bring everything to completion.

Questions for Reflection:

- When God answers prayers, which answer is easiest to accept? Which is hardest?

  _____

  _____

  _____

  _____

- Who is Jesus to you? What words would you use to describe him?

  _____

  _____

  _____

  _____

- Where do you see Emmanuel- God with us- present in your life?

_____

_____

_____

_____

Journaling space:

A Prayer of Presence

Lord, you have always been with me.
I can see your works throughout my life,
leading me to this place.
bringing me back to you whenever I stray.
There is nothing I can do to repay you.
I give you my life, Lord.
Use me as you will.
Help me to be open to the needs of others
and to respond to their weakness with compassion:
the same compassion you have shown me.
May I be a rock in the storm for them.
May my actions bring them to you.
Amen.

Scripture: Second Reading

ROMANS 16: 25-27 – CYCLE B

Now to him who can strengthen you, according to my gospel and the proclamation of Jesus Christ, according to the revelation of the mystery kept secret for long ages but now manifested through the prophetic writings and, according to the command of the eternal God, made known to all nations to bring about the obedience of faith, to the only wise God, through Jesus Christ be glory forever and ever. Amen.

Lectio Divina:

- Invite the Holy Spirit to be with you.
- **Lectio:** What word or phrase stands out?
- **Meditatio:** What is God saying to you today?

- **Oratio:** What do you have to say to God? How will your life change because of this passage?
- **Contemplatio:** thank God in silence.

Questions for Reflection:

- How does your life glorify God?

  _____

  _____

  _____

  _____

- How has God given you strength this season?

  _____

  _____

  _____

  _____

- How has Scripture been a source of strength and clarity to you throughout Advent?

  _____

  _____

  _____

  _____

Belonging

One of the gifts I'll never take for granted is the gift of belonging.

At a summer camp in elementary school, during cabin time, we each had to go around and share what our greatest fear was. I wasn't afraid of spiders, or heights, or ghosties. I surprised myself when I said, "rejection." It was true then, I realized, and it's still true today.

My greatest desire is belonging.

As a child, it manifested in making friends and play dates with my classmates. It manifested in playtime with my cousins out at my grandparent's farm.

As a teen, it took roots in deeper friendships, and relationships with boys- young men- and in seeking out a college where I would fit.

It's the reason it took me 26 years to write and publish my first book.

I was blessed to find a home in my faith community in college, but I never stopped seeking. My life became a whirlwind of transitions when I graduated: I got married, started a job, and did the long-distance relationship thing with my husband while he finished training. And then we moved to Alaska.

I had never realized how much belonging I'd connected to my hometown until I had to leave it. I had all the same fears that I'd begun with: would I find any friends in Alaska? How would my husband and I do, alone, together, away from family? Where would I work? Who would be a part of my community? It hurt to leave my family and those I loved,

God knows us, and he gives us peace in ways that fulfill us. He gave me everything I needed for belonging in Alaska: community, connectedness, and all the comforts of home. I can't list all the people who have made Alaska home for me; it would never be complete. But I'll share one story. One of the greatest senses of belonging I felt was at my husband's going-away party for his deployment.

It was a small little gathering of five friends, but looking back, I realize that it represented everything I'd been seeking: new friends, rooted in faith, connected through work and community. They loved me, and they loved my husband... even if we'd only been here a pair of years.

One of our closest friends has a certain intensity about him: he loves, and well, and isn't afraid to show it.

As we toasted my husband, our friend good-naturedly threatened him within an inch of his life that he had better come back, for the love of all things holy.

It was through that encounter, and many others, that God manifested a sense of peace in my life. God places people in our lives when we need them most. There are a hundred other stories like this one, and I'm sure we each have impactful people that make a world of difference when we need them most. We are each loved by God, and we each have community. Even in the darkest storms of life and the most intimidating transitions of life, God will send us people. May he also grant us the courage to be that person to others in their time of need.

Questions for Reflection:

- Have you ever experienced a transition where you had to rediscover who you are and where you belong? How have you changed and grown because of the transition?

  _____

  _____

  _____

  _____

- Who are the people who influence you most? Where do you feel a sense of belonging?

_____

_____

_____

_____

- How does your faith contribute to your sense of belonging?

_____

_____

_____

_____

Journaling space:

_____

_____

_____

_____

_____

_____

_____

_____

_____

_____

Scripture: Gospel

LUKE 1: 26-38 – CYCLE B

In the sixth month, the angel Gabriel was sent from God to a town of Galilee called Nazareth, to a virgin betrothed to a man named Joseph, of the house of David, and the virgin's name was Mary. And coming to her, he said, "Hail, favored one! The Lord is with you." But she was greatly troubled at what was said and pondered what sort of greeting this might be. Then the angel said to her, "Do not be afraid, Mary, for you have found favor with God. Behold, you will conceive in your womb and bear a son, and you shall name him Jesus. He will be great and will be called Son of the Most High, and the Lord God will give him the throne of David his father, and he will rule over the house of Jacob forever, and of his kingdom there will be no end." But Mary said to the angel, "How can this be, since I have no relations with a man?" And the angel said to her in reply, "The holy Spirit will come upon you, and the power of the Most High will overshadow you. Therefore the child to be born will be called holy, the Son of God. And behold, Elizabeth, your relative, has also conceived a son in her old age, and this is the sixth month for her who was called barren; for nothing will be impossible for God." Mary said, "Behold, I am the handmaid of the Lord. May it be done to me according to your word." Then the angel departed from her.

Lectio Divina:

- Invite the Holy Spirit to be with you.
- **Lectio:** What word or phrase stands out?
- **Meditatio:** What is God saying to you today?
- **Oratio:** What do you have to say to God? How will your life change because of this passage?
- **Contemplatio:** thank God in silence.

Questions for Reflection:

- If you were in Mary's shoes, how would you have felt about Gabriel's message? What questions would you have asked him?

_____

_____

_____

_____

- Think of a time you received unexpected news. How did it impact you? Were you able to find God's presence in the situation?

_____

_____

_____

_____

- Have you ever doubted God or his ability to work miracles? Where has God surprised you in your life?

_____

_____

_____

_____

Incarnation

Think of the worst household chore you have on your list. The one you hate the very most. The one that makes you crazy. The one that you avoid as often as possible, for as long as possible.

For me, it's the dishes. I don't know how I got stuck being responsible for them, but some days, it seems like they will be the death of me. They pile up faster than I expect and they're never all done at the same time. And sometimes, they're gross. Then the chore becomes twice as fun.

Sometimes I behave like my students who get squeamish during a messy project. I love hosting pumpkin carving events. Every year, it amazes me how many teenagers refuse to put their hand inside a pumpkin. I remind them that skin is waterproof. Whatever gross thing you're about to touch, it will wash off. And yes, you can go wash your hands. But finish gutting your pumpkin first, please and thank you.

Lucky for us, God wasn't afraid to get his hands dirty.

The fact of the Incarnation is mind-blowing. God, the creator, the ultimate perfect person, sent his Son into a broken, messy world. We don't get it right. We are a hopeless mess on our own. But God has never wanted to leave us alone.

I am overwhelmed by God's relentless love for us. God came down. He loved us so much that he became human. He entered into the messiness that is human life. Think of all the brokenness in your circle of life. That's what God chooses to enter into. He doesn't hesitate; he comes into the world and dwells there with us, amidst it all. He came here for us, and he was crucified on our behalf, so we can be reunited with him in eternity.

He paid the ultimate price. But first, he became one of us. He was not afraid of the mess.

Through his incarnation, death, and resurrection, he has made us sons and daughters of his kingdom. No matter the condition of our human family, we are- and always will be- children of God. We are beloved by our Father beyond our greatest imaginings.

As this Advent draws to a close and we encounter Christ this Christmas, let's choose to love. Let's choose peace in a world of transitions. Let's choose joy, faith, and hope, in a world that promises all those things, but cannot fulfill them. Let's turn to Christ, the one who can satisfy our deepest desires.

Today, let's ask for the grace to encounter Christ on Christmas. Even in the little things, our God is faithful. He will come to us, if we open ourselves to him.

Questions for Reflection:

- How has God been present in the messiness of your life?

_____

_____

_____

_____

- Where have you felt God's incarnate presence this Advent season? What has he taught you?

_____

_____

_____

_____

- How will you choose peace this week?

_____

_____

Encounter:

_____

_____

Journaling space:

_____

_____

_____

_____

_____

_____

_____

_____

_____

_____

_____

_____

_____

_____

_____

_____

Week 4 Check-in

Week 4 is complete, and Easter is upon us! Congratulations on completing this journey.

- Look back to your Week 3 Check-in (page 117) and your Pre-Advent Check-in (page 28). How have you grown this Advent?

  _____

  _____

  _____

  _____

- Where has God been working in your life?

  _____

  _____

_____

_____

- How did you give back to the community this season? Which way was your favorite?

_____

_____

_____

_____

- What Advent traditions did you try? Which one do you plan to continue next Advent?

_____

_____

_____

_____

- Other Reflections:

_____

_____

_____

_____

Before you go to Christmas Mass this week:

- Who/what will you pray for?

_____

_____

_____

_____

- Christmas Homily Notes:

_____

_____

_____

_____

Journaling space:

_____

_____

_____

_____

_____

_____

_____

_____

_____

Christmas: Encounter

Advent is over. Our moment is here: Christ has come. Our long-awaited Savoir is with us.

And this last chapter is not mine to write.

I've shared my stories, my reflections, my questions. I have made space in my life for Christ, and if you've read this far, I know you've made space in your life, too. You've given him time; that's one gift we won't always have. We have to make the best of it.

We each encounter Christ at Mass on Christmas, and through our families and friends. But as I said at the beginning of this book: I'm not providing a magic bullet. I'm giving guidelines. The rest is up to you and Jesus. Where will you go from here? How is God calling us to continuous conversion? What does he ask of us? These are questions I can't answer for you. I can only answer them for me. All I can say this: take courage. Be not afraid. He is with us. He is always with us.

Thank you for joining me on this journey of faith this Advent.

May the hope, faith, joy, and peace of Christ remain with you and yours, this Christmas season and always.

Questions for Reflection:

- How did you encountered Christ this Advent?

_____

_____

_____

_____

- How has this Advent been different for you?

_____

_____

_____

_____

- How will you continue to grow in faith throughout this Christmas season?

_____

_____

_____

Notes

Encounter:

About the Author

Anna Schulten is a cradle Catholic who lives in Anchorage, Alaska with her husband, dog, cat, and assorted fish. She is most definitely a cat person.

Though she has dreamed of being a published author since kindergarten and has written articles for various Catholic newspapers, this is her first book.

Made in the USA
Lexington, KY
19 October 2017